The Road to Bethlehem
Musings on the Coming King

CELESTE ALLEN

Copyright ©2014 Celeste Allen

All rights reserved. No part of this publication may be reproduced in any form without written permission from the author.

Scripture taken from The Holy Bible, New International Version® (NIV®), Copyright ©1973, 1978, 1984 by International Bible Society. All rights reserved worldwide.

Etymologies are taken from Online Etymology Dictionary (http://www.etymonline.com)

Jesus Calling, Sarah Young, copyright ©2004, Thomas Nelson. Nashville, Tennessee. All rights reserved. Used by permission.

Enchanted April, Elizabeth von Arnim, copyright ©1922, MacMillan and Co. Ltd., Great Britain. All rights reserved.

Charles Elliot. "Just As I Am." Public Domain.

John Newton. "Amazing Grace." Public Domain.

Charles Wesley. "O For a Thousand Tongues." Public Domain.

One Thousand Gifts by Ann Voskamp, copyright ©2010, Zondervan, Grand Rapids, Michigan. Used by permission of Zondervan. www.zondervan.com.

Frances Ridley Havergal. "Take My Life and Let It Be." Public Domain.

ISBN: 1502913801
ISBN-13: 978-1502913807

DEDICATION

To all those who have walked with me during these twenty-five years of ministry. I can never say, "Thank you" enough.

CONTENTS

	Acknowledgements	i
	Preface	iii
1	Anticipation	1
2	Adventure	3
3	Telling the Truth	5
4	Fear Not	7
5	But How?	9
6	Stubborn Joy	11
7	Delayed Gratification	13
8	Open Hands	15
9	Inconceivable	17
10	Without a Doubt	19
11	Welcome	21
12	Home for the Holidays	23
13	Tell It Like It Is	25
14	Expectation	27
15	Action	29
16	Gate Crashers	31
17	Here and Now	33
18	Thinking It Through	35
19	Traveling Mercies	37
20	Coming and Going	39
21	Eyes Wide Open	41
22	Step by Step	43
23	Miracles	45
24	Open Arms	47
25	O Happy Day	49
	About the Author	51

ACKNOWLEDGMENTS

Thanks to all those who support the work of The Oaks Oasis. Without you I would not be here in Italy, and if I weren't here, this book would never have been written. I raise my teacup to Sue Erikson for encouraging me in writing meditations. Hats off to Carol Christensen for stepping out of her faith comfort zone to edit this work. (*Mazel tov*, my friend!) And finally, special thanks to Mary Huff for, well, everything.

PREFACE

The road to Bethlehem is not long, only eighty miles from Mary and Joseph's home town of Nazareth. And yet Christ's journey to birth is vast. The trip started in Eden, continued through Mount Moriah, took a side step into Moab, got waylaid into Babylon and settled in Nazareth before finally ending in a manger. It's a journey from innocence through sacrifice and suffering, confusion and rebellion. Ah, but it ends in redemption, in joy. The story of Jesus' coming to earth began when God promised the serpent's demise in Genesis 3, but the Advent narrative begins thousands of years later, the moment the angel appears to Zechariah.

These meditations are my journey through the story of Jesus' first coming. Some are personal, some universal. Some look directly at the events described in the Bible; others focus more on our lives here and now. Each day as I follow the thread of my thoughts, eventually I come to a point at which I am led to a prayer. You may want to join me in my prayer, or you may be inspired to pray a prayer your own.

On a practical note, Advent runs from the fourth Sunday before Christmas through Christmas Eve. Thus the number of days can vary from twenty-four to twenty-eight. For the sake of simplicity I've created meditations to begin on the first of December, ending with Christmas Day.

If your tradition has never included celebrating the Advent season, I encourage you to enjoy taking a few moments each day to contemplate thoughts about the season and the events that led up to Christ's birth. If Advent has been a regular part of your faith calendar, I hope you enjoy what may be a different look at the season. In either case, I invite you to join me in the following pages as I walk the road to Bethlehem.

Celeste Allen
Porano, Italy
November 2014

DAY ONE: ANTICIPATION

Anticipate – from Latin anticipatus, "take (care of) ahead of time," literally "taking into possession beforehand"

Christmas is coming, and I'm thrilled. I've been looking forward to decorating, to carols, to visitors. I'm excited thinking about menu planning and putting up the tree.

I love giving gifts. This year I'm in a place with few friends, none of whom I feel close enough to exchange presents with. Yet I'm wanting to bake breads and cookies, make jams and spiced and sugared nuts and nestle them all in lovingly decorated baskets wrapped in colorful cellophane and bright ribbons.

I'm longing to make wreaths and drape garland and glean pine boughs. To light candles and make eggnog and mull wine. Like a child again, I'm yearning to surround myself with wrapping paper and bows and tinsel.

What's missing? Family, friends, traditions. It's true none of those are here, but… What's missing?

Jesus.

All my anticipation has been wrapped around the trappings of Christmas. Good things all, lovely and pure and beautiful.

Yet I find myself caught up in the good things while forgetting the best thing. I long to long for the truth of Christmas. A manger in the shadow of a cross, a family far from home bringing into being a Spirit-child far from heaven.

What I want is to want Him, the Christ at the heart of Christmas. I want to anticipate Jesus with the root meaning of the word "anticipation": I want my heart to take possession of Him before He arrives.

God created joy. He gave us wonder, and when I take a childlike delight in the fun and beauty of the western traditions of Christmas, that is a blessing and a prayer to Him. But what most fills His heart with rapture is when I take childlike delight in Him.

So in the midst of my anticipation, my prayer is to look forward to Jesus, to prepare my heart for His coming and to see His hand in each tray of cookies, His heart in every wreath, His life shining in every candle. That will bless Him, and it will bless me, too.

Finally, brothers and sisters, whatever is true, whatever is noble, whatever is right, whatever is pure, whatever is lovely, whatever is admirable—if anything is excellent or praiseworthy—think about such things. – Philippians 4:8

DAY TWO: ADVENTURE

Adventure – from Latin adventura (res) *"(a thing) about to happen"*

This coming event, this thing about to happen, Jesus *in utero*, preparing to burst onto the scene with angels and shooting stars, a cosmic event in every sense of the word—it all begins so quietly. In those nine silent months as cells split and organs form, as the Holy Spirit child grows from a simple "be it unto me" into a fingered, toed, blinking God-man, Mary silently ponders these things in her heart. The child is already inside her; the child is yet to come. And with His coming, Mary is about to live the greatest adventure ever imagined.

Yes, the angel Gabriel has told her the child will be *called* the Son of God. But does she understand that this "thing about to happen" will be God Himself? God clothed in soft baby flesh, half-blind and helpless, lullabied to sleep in her arms.

As she looks forward, already possessing a miracle in her womb, already having taken hold of mystery, does even an inkling stir of the amazing things she will witness? The next thirty-three years will be a rollercoaster of joy and confusion and astonishment and soul-wrenching grief. The adventure laid out before her will make history. Does Mary realize she will rock the babe who will rock the world?

Does she realize the adventure will continue centuries after the body that birthed this Mystery has turned to dust? Because this adventure comes to everyone who takes hold of the mystery. Each day is a looking forward, each moment an arrival at some place only God can take us. Every breath is "a thing about to happen."

So Advent leads us into adventure. The cosmic event of Jesus' arrival is an hourly occurrence if we allow it to be. Does my heart yearn to hold in my arms what God has promised? Do I quietly ponder His words to me? In my looking forward do I look for the face of God?

I admit most of my time is spent looking down: at the food I'm cooking, at the floor I'm mopping, at the screen where my words are appearing. I want to join Mary in looking inward at what God has said, looking forward toward the adventure that is life with God.

My prayer today is to see the adventure of Advent, to see God's coming in my cooking and my cleaning and my communicating. Jesus is coming. Jesus is here.

Day and night they never stop saying: "Holy, holy, holy is the Lord God Almighty, who was, and is, and is to come." – Revelation 4:8

DAY THREE: TELLING THE TRUTH

Truth – from triewe, treowe *"faithful"*

This story is so well known, even to those who don't accept it: a man and a woman, a donkey, a star, shepherds with their sheep, three kings. We forget that the myth is not the true story.

There is no mention of a donkey; the shepherds *left* their flocks. The timing is not explicit, but it's stated that Mary and Joseph were already in Bethlehem when Jesus' birth occurred—probably no birth pangs on the very day of their arrival. And by the time the wise men arrived (not kings and number unspecified) the family had found a house to live in. So even the familiar time-trodden story we picture is false.

And there is nothing quaint or idyllic about the reality. The night was almost certainly not silent. Bethlehem was chock-full of travelers. More likely the air was filled with the clamor of voices and the calls of animals. No wonder the angels appeared to shepherds in the fields. Could anyone have even heard the angelic chorus over the noise of the overcrowded streets of Bethlehem?

All this to say, sometimes what is familiar is not what is

true. Sometimes truth is a tiny nugget buried under the layers of presumption and storytelling and wishful thinking.

We are all—even the least imaginative of us—fictionalizers. We are all—even the most pragmatic of us—romantics. But sometimes truth belies the romantic, fictitious overlay. Sometimes truth is a noisy, smelly, crowed place, cold with the night air whistling through loose wall boards or stuffy with the press of animal bodies.

Maybe truth isn't the misty, sepia-tinted picture we've come to accept, but it is, instead, a dimly-lit room or the bright, harsh light of mid-day. Whatever the case, the beauty is not in the myth. The beauty is in the truth. The truth of God-with-us, the Christ child, the baby and the King. The truth is there in beauty, there in glory and wonder.

My prayer today is that I will see truth and love the beauty in the truth, whatever that truth is.

So Jesus was saying to those Jews who had believed Him, "If you continue in My word, then you are truly disciples of Mine; and you will know the truth, and the truth will make you free." – John 8:31-32

DAY FOUR:
FEAR NOT

Fear – from Proto-Indo-European verbal root *per- "to try, risk," related to *per- "forward, through"

Angels are not to be toyed with. Neither chubby babies with tiny, gossamer wings nor shimmering asexual humans with faint golden haloes, real angels are clearly terrifying. Nearly every time an angel shows up in the Bible, its first words are "Don't be afraid."

Bearing this in mind, the angelic encounters in the Advent narrative take on a somewhat different slant from how we normally think of them. Imagine Zechariah, basking in the privilege and glory of entering the temple with no thought but to light the incense, when suddenly a fearsome creature stands before him. Imagine young Mary, perhaps going about her household chores or walking home from the market, when a terrifying being appears. Imagine Joseph, in deep turmoil over the presumed infidelity of his fiancée, waking from a fitful sleep after a dream encounter with this creature. Imagine simple shepherds, trying to stay awake lest a threat appears to their flock, when suddenly a far bigger threat appears in the sky. Yet each time the angel says, "Don't be afraid."

And the angels are only the beginning of things fearful. In the beauty of the quaintly familiar story it's easy to forget that the whole situation from start to finish had to be frightening. Elderly Elizabeth and Zechariah are faced with the fearsome prospect of raising a child—a very special child. Mary will surely become the object of coarse speculation and Joseph the butt of ridicule. These things are fears of what is to come, but there were also the immediate and real causes for fear. Mary was giving birth for the first time—surrounded by animals, for crying out loud! Did she have anyone to attend to her except Joseph? Was even the innkeeper's wife there?

There is much, so much, to fear in life. Yet Jesus tells us, His little flock, to fear not, commands us not to be anxious as if the most natural reaction in the world could be controlled. And so perhaps it can. We cannot calm our fears by sheer force of will. But we can control our reactions through a steady focus on the One who is in charge. If our eyes are locked on the coming King, the One who is greater than any threat, then we will see the Conqueror, not the peril.

Mary understood this when she said "Be it unto me according to Your will." Whatever the challenges that might accompany what God asked of her, they would never be as big as the God who asked it. Perhaps this is what it means when it says that she pondered things in her heart. She laid her potential fears before her Lord and then turned them over and around in the light of His greatness.

My prayer today is that I would look at every circumstance, every challenge, every situation that comes to me in the light of the Light of the world so that I would know there is never any reason to fear.

But the angel said to them, "Do not be afraid. I bring you good news that will cause great joy for all the people." – Luke 2:10

DAY FIVE:
BUT HOW?

Don't let your need to understand distract you from my presence – Sarah Young, Jesus Calling

Mary, young, devout, woman of God. When the angel Gabriel came to you announcing miraculous news of the impossible, you asked—as anyone would—"How can this be?" Joseph, man of integrity and compassion, when you learned of your fiancée's pregnancy and the angel spoke into your dreams an incomprehensible explanation, you could not help but wonder. Elizabeth, long-suffering wife, when your husband brought you words of laughable absurdity, at best you must have looked askance. Zechariah, faithful servant of the Lord, when the Spirit spoke a truth beyond belief, you, you alone in this astonishing adventure, replied in unbelief. You alone were more struck by incredulity than by awe at the God who declared this good news to you.

God-with-us is miracle. His intervention, stepping out of eternity to join the squalor and disorder and glory that His creation had become, is, frankly, mind blowing. God suspends the laws He created for His universe in order to reach out to us, to me. Do I dare place Him in a neat little box that fits my understanding? Do I dismiss His working because I can't think my way through His logic? Do I focus on good sense? Or do I, like Mary, Joseph and Elizabeth, simply accept what I do not understand and revel in the reality that God chooses to act in *my* life, to look at me, to be with me?

This Advent adventure bristles with miracles, with intrusions of the divine into the mundane. There is so much to be in awe of. Yet the most awesome aspect of this adventure is God *with* us. God present to His beloved people. This is glory and joy and wonder. This is comfort and love. God present in Spirit and in flesh, incomprehensible but true.

My prayer today is that I will bask in God's presence, however He shows Himself.

But God chose the foolish things of the world to shame the wise; God chose the weak things of the world to shame the strong. – 1 Corinthians 1:27

DAY SIX: STUBBORN JOY

Surmount – from Old French surmonter *"rise above," from* sur- *"beyond"* + monter *"to go up"*

Where does teeth-gritted perseverance fall in our waiting, our joyous anticipation? Jesus came to give abundant life—and abundant life we have. Yet sometimes the manifestations of abundant life can be rather different from what we expect.

Joy is what the angels proclaimed, great joy. But joy doesn't always look like grinning, carefree skipping through life. Joy is a choice, sometimes a hard choice, sometimes in the face of overwhelming opposition, of pain or grief or all the nastiness life can throw at us. Joy is a choice to give thanks, to seek God, to grasp tight to the promise that He is with us—even when we don't see Him. To cling to the hope that He is the God who was and is and is to come.

Sometimes white-knuckled hope is the best hope of all. It is hope headstrong in the face of the onslaught. And when that hope is fulfilled the satisfaction is far sweeter than the fulfillment of mild, untested hope.

Joy is not heaven on earth. Heaven will never inhabit a fallen world. But joy is in the hope that the coming King is

God-with-us. He is here in Spirit and will come in flesh again and make all things right.

Until then, joy is a stubborn choice based in truth, rooted in Advent hope. We wait for the baby, for the King. We anticipate the day when in a twinkling we will be changed—all things will be changed. Our Advent waiting prefigures that final waiting. And that is a hope that will not disappoint.

My prayer today is that I would cling to Advent hope, Advent joy in the face of what seem like insurmountable obstacles.

Not only so, but we also glory in our sufferings, because we know that suffering produces perseverance; perseverance, character; and character, hope. And hope does not put us to shame, because God's love has been poured out into our hearts through the Holy Spirit, who has been given to us. – Romans 5:3-5

DAY SEVEN:
DELAYED GRATIFICATION

Delay – from Old French delaiier, *from* de- *"away, from"* + laier *"leave, let"*

Waiting. Some tolerate it better than others, but no one likes it. Advent speaks to the restless heart, the soul that seeks and yearns but does not yet possess. Nine long months Mary waited for Jesus' birth. We wait only four weeks in the Advent season. In some stores in the US Christmas decorations show up in September. This somehow seems more like an obscenity than Christmas spirit. Here in Italy it is unheard of to put up decorations before December eighth. So, while I put up my tree and a row of indoor bulbs on the first day of Advent, I've dutifully delayed putting up further decorations. Lights, bulbs, wreaths lie in wait. I weave grape vines, winding them into circlets to be decorated with berries, rosehips and the dried husks of wildflowers from the garden.

But this waiting to decorate, waiting for December eighth, waiting for my first December guests to arrive, this waiting is all prelude to and conjoined with the waiting for the manger to be filled. Waiting for God-with-us to be made manifest in the flesh, in my heart.

The delay is part of the preparation. I feel the lack, feel the need, the void where I want Him to be but where He is not yet. I long for Him to fill that space, and yet I must wait. Weeping may last the night, but joy comes in the morning. How I long for that glorious, festive morning, that Christmas morning when the manger of my heart will be filled with the Christ child. His arrival in me, His arrival back in the world.

My prayer today is that God will use this waiting time to prepare my heart to welcome Him. To sweep out the dust and cobwebs, clean the old grain out of the manger and create in me a resting place fit for a King.

Create in me a pure heart, O God, and renew a steadfast spirit within me. – Psalm 51:10

DAY EIGHT: OPEN HANDS

There's nothing left to it. We're in God's hands now! – Elizabeth von Arnim, Enchanted April

Walking into this adventure of anticipation, I want to map it out. I want to see what's coming, figure out how to apprehend it both before and when it arrives. I say that I want to grab hold of this advent adventure in order to ride the wave of its blessing. Really, I want to be in charge of it.

And yet I am by nature a contradiction: both a planner and a "fly by the seat of the pants kind of girl." I write up exhaustive menus; I make precise shopping lists; I time my meal preparation down to five-minute intervals. And I switch recipes at the last minute, add and subtract items from my list willy-nilly, decide that I can start earlier or later than planned.

So part of me wants to control the adventure, and part of me says, "Go with whatever comes." I like to see this as being willing to flow with the Spirit. In reality, it may just be another disguise of control. Because in choosing to flow with it, I am still in charge, and I am choosing to be flexible.

At any given moment, we like to think we know what's going on and are in control of our lives. We think there is security in the job that pays our bills, the loved ones who affirm our value, the schedule we set for our days. In reality, it's Job's lot. Our livelihood, loved ones and calendars can be swept away in a blink. We are never in control. Never. When nature goes awry we call it an "act of God" as if it's not an act of God when things go well. When we lose control we claim that "we are in God's hands now" as if we weren't in God's hands before.

The coming King, the babe in Mary's womb, the risen Christ holds our days and hours and seconds. How can I look forward to this coming, anticipating His reign in my life while still walking through the events that He unfolds in my life? How do I grasp the God who is and is to come? I want to hold lightly to the things He gives me, the people and events and gifts He brings into my life, but hold tight to Him. I want to look for His fingerprints and follow His invisible footsteps into whatever path He sets out before me. To hear His whisper so I can respond with my "be it unto me" even if He asks the impossible, even if He holds out Job's lot for me to take.

And so my prayer today, as I struggle to let God be God, is that I will hold this adventure with open hands, listening to the Lord and relying on Him to guide every step, every word, every thought.

Whether you turn to the right or to the left, your ears will hear a voice behind you, saying, "This is the way; walk in it." – Isaiah 30:21

DAY NINE:
INCONCEIVABLE

Inconceivable – from in- "not, opposite of" + conceivable; from Latin concipere *"to take in and hold; become pregnant," from* com-, + capere *"to take," from* kap- *"to grasp"*

This thing to come, this God-with-us is truly beyond imagining. The Christ child in Mary's womb, a Being conceived of Spirit and made flesh, grows, changes, becomes complete. A flesh child is mind-boggling enough, but a God-made-flesh child? And this Spirit Being comes to live in me, too? It is more than the mind can hold. I'm glad my mind does not have to hold it, that my spirit and this Spirit can commune without my understanding.

We know little of Mary. A simple girl, likely not educated beyond the basics of making a home, of cooking, cleaning, keeping a garden, haggling at the market. But most certainly she is well-learned in the art of loving God with heart, soul and strength. She may not have been able to quote chapter and verse of the Law and Prophets, but God did not see her as lacking in any way. Her mind did not need to grasp the thing God asked. She need know only enough to accept and wait and ponder. A heart to accept, a womb to accept, Mary was fit to conceive the One who would be the way, the truth and the life because she loved the One who gives life.

I struggle to understand the hows and whys. I tussle with concepts and grapple with ideas. I study the Greek and the Hebrew in search of clarity. I grope and probe until I feel as though my head will explode. All I really need is to take in and hold the truth, the reality of the Christ child. The only thing I truly need to ponder is the enormity of God's love, that He would send His Son, Himself to this outlet of hell, this adjunct of heaven to live and die and live again because of His inconceivable love for His creation, His children, me. This is enough, this is too much. This is pondering enough for a lifetime.

My prayer today is that I will let God's immensity be and simply focus on His love.

I do not concern myself with great matters or things too wonderful for me. But I have calmed and quieted myself, I am like a weaned child with its mother; like a weaned child I am content. – Psalm 131:1(b)-2

DAY TEN:
WITHOUT A DOUBT

Just as I am, though tossed about with many a conflict, many a doubt –
Charles Elliot, "Just As I Am"

There's one in every crowd. In the whole of the Advent adventure only Zechariah doubted—not for long, mind you, but he did try to apply logic when God presented a miracle. I think that's why I like him. Zechariah is so real. It's not that the other players in this story aren't genuine. It's just that they all seem so unflappable. Certainly that's not a bad thing. A jog through the Old Testament shows that God has a long history of dealing with people who question His words. So kudos to all those who accepted the angelic proclamations on face value.

Ah, but Zechariah. Luke tells us "Both of them [Zechariah and Elizabeth] were righteous in the sight of God, observing all the Lord's commands and decrees blamelessly." It wasn't that Zechariah was prone to disobedience or faithlessness. He was just having a very human moment in the midst of a spiritual life. Just as we all do.

It's as if God chose Zechariah just to remind us that the story is true. In a morality play everyone would blithely acquiesce, believing whatever God laid before them in order to show how things are supposed to go, to show that good people always hear and accept. In real life there's always someone who needs a little convincing, some good person, chosen by God, who needs some reassurance. Whether Moses, Gideon or Thomas, there was one in every crowd. And it's Zechariah in the Advent crowd.

We all can be a little like Zechariah, living out lives that basically glorify God but occasionally letting our logical, human minds sow seeds of doubt about God's call, proclamations or actions. God may not send an angel to strike us mute because of our questionings. But He will, in some way, tap us on the shoulder to remind us that He is God, and He can do miracles without our permission or understanding, thank you.

My prayer today is that I will heed God's call—or at least heed His shoulder tap—and walk in faith for whatever He calls me to.

Gideon replied, "If now I have found favor in your eyes, give me a sign that it is really you talking to me." – Judges 6:17

DAY ELEVEN: WELCOME

Welcome – Old English from earlier wilcuma *(n.) "welcome guest," literally "one whose coming is in accord with another's will," from* willa *"pleasure, desire, choice"* + cuma *"guest"*

How do you welcome a baby? How do you welcome a king? Both occasions are auspicious, both life changing. And when the two are combined, world changing. Hearts swell at the news, faces break into enormous smiles of joy.

A baby, much less a king, is sometimes a scheduled guest, but as often as not, he comes unbidden, at the time of his own choosing. As soon as we know he's coming we begin to create a special place for this guest. We clean and prepare, buy new accoutrements to make our guest comfortable, to show how pleased we are at his arrival. All must be made ready and perfect.

So how do I usher this most special guest into my life? How do I open my home, open my arms, open my life to this coming King? How can I sweep out the guest room of my heart? How can I move myself into the guest room and give the master bedroom to my guest—my Master? How do I prepare my heart home to receive this One whose coming I anticipate with joy? Because His coming is my desire, my pleasure, and so much in accordance with my will.

As I decorate my house, so I must decorate my heart—but not with baubles and excesses. Rather, I will decorate my heart with simplicity, taking away rather than adding to. Let my heart become quieter as my house becomes noisier. Tear away the glitter and pretense as I string tinsel and hang bulbs. As I deck the halls of my home I will strip the halls of my heart. Made bare and unadorned, my heart will become the perfect manger for this coming King.

How do you welcome a baby? How do you welcome a king? You open your eyes and your heart and become your barest, truest self. This is the greatest welcome.

My prayer today is to become simplicity itself that my Lord will feel the welcome I so wish to give.

For this is what the high and exalted One says—he who lives forever, whose name is holy: "I live in a high and holy place, but also with the one who is contrite and lowly in spirit, to revive the spirit of the lowly and to revive the heart of the contrite." – Isaiah 57:15

DAY TWELVE:
HOME FOR THE HOLIDAYS

'Tis grace hath brought me safe thus far, and grace will lead me home –
John Newton, "Amazing Grace"

Something about Christmas calls us home, calls us to the people and places that sooth the soul. We want the familiar, the understood, the known. The joys of hearth and home, the embraces of loving family, time-honored traditions filled with the cheer of friends and familiar places.

Christmas invokes images of toasty kitchens full of glorious, homey smells, of cookies and pies and gingerbread men. The clean scent of pine, the crisp green and sparkling red of holly, sounds of crunching snow and tinkling bells. It is all so well-known and comforting.

And yet that first Christmas, before traditions, there was no comforting bosom of home and family. There were animal smells and sounds, strangers coming and going. And the infant King, fresh introduced to His earthly family, had begun His adventure not with a coming, but with a leaving. He had left His home nine months before to journey to a strange and perilous land. From the home of heaven, via the security of the womb, to the noise and light and terror of life on this earth. It is no wonder babies cry when they're born! How much more so this babe, who stepped down from heaven, perfect communion, to enter a world of insecurity, of separation, of isolation where no home is as complete, no embrace as total as that of the Father?

Yet the coming King chose to leave His home and come into ours, come *back* to ours. His leave-taking was also a homecoming, returning to walk in the garden in the cool of the day with those He had created. Returning to redeem that garden, that creation, and bring it back to what it was meant to be.

In a way He brought His home with Him. For surely home is where the Father is, and the Christ child was one with the Father even in His separation here on earth. And so home is where He is for us as well. Living in Him means we are always home.

My prayer today is that I will know my home in Him so intimately that it will not matter where I am, for in Him I will always be home for the holidays.

This is how God showed his love among us: He sent his one and only Son into the world that we might live through him. – 1 John 4:9

DAY THIRTEEN: TELL IT LIKE IT IS

My gracious Master and my God, assist me to proclaim and spread through all the earth abroad the honors of thy Name – Charles Wesley, "O For a Thousand Tongues"

There's a funny juxtaposition in the New Testament. Jesus regularly gave explicit instructions to not tell anyone who He was or what He'd done. Not always, but often enough to be noteworthy. It's as if He wanted to keep His Christ-hood a secret. And when He finally did declare it, well, all hell broke loose. (John 8:58-59, Matthew 26:64-66)

Now compare that to Jesus' arrival on earth. Angels start popping up everywhere to herald the news. Strangers come from far and near, the word is spread, stars nova, angels sing. All heaven breaks loose.

I wonder what those early days of Jesus' infancy were like? It's not as if the shepherds' visit went unnoticed. Scripture tells us they spread the news of what the angel had told them and had the town buzzing. Did Mary and Joseph achieve instant celebrity status? Did everyone want to get close, see this baby phenomenon, buy a cup of coffee for the lucky parents? (At least until the family quietly slipped away to Egypt. But that's another story.)

Two simple people from a backwater village suddenly thrust into the center of God's big story. Yet aren't we there, too? Simple people going about our simple lives until God breaks into our stories, entrusting us with the knowledge of His Son, asking us to incarnate His life in the world around us, to walk in faith in the midst of sometimes staggering circumstances.

Are you sometimes tempted to keep it a secret? I am. How many times have I sat on an airplane, hoping no one would sit next to me? How many times have I chosen not to tell someone I would pray for him. How many times have I refrained from incarnating God's life to those around me for fear of all hell breaking loose? When, in fact, for all I know all heaven might have broken loose instead.

My prayer today is that I will celebrate Jesus' celebrity whenever and wherever God prompts me to do so.

For the creation waits in eager expectation for the children of God to be revealed. – Romans 8:19

DAY FOURTEEN: EXPECTATION

Imagine – from Latin imaginari *"to form a mental picture to oneself"*

Looking forward, we hope for something new, desired yet unimagined, something we envision but can't put our finger on. We hope for we know not what. The wise men knew the star foretold the birth of a king. In expectation they set out on an adventure, searching for a royal bedchamber. Instead they found a humble house. Perhaps they were surprised, but they were not disappointed. They presented their gifts, they worshipped, they found the King they'd been looking for.

This Advent adventure is filled with expectation and surprise. We know what's coming: Christmas pageants, Advent candles, carols, crowds. It is all very familiar. Yet at the same time the anticipation is new each year, and—if we allow it—the joy fresh. We know what we are expecting, but God so often adds a twist that can leave us breathless with surprise.

The joy of expectation lies both in imagining what we await and believing it will be something more, something greater than what we imagine. We know, but we don't know. It may seem there is nothing new under the sun, and yet God says He will do a new thing—and we must wait for it.

Why the pleasure in taking out the same old decorations and decking the halls in the same old way? Because it heralds something more. The hope is for a gift greater than anything found under a tree. The expectation is the new arrival—once again—of the coming King.

My prayer today is to focus on the hope that does not disappoint, the hope of the King who was and is and is to come.

See, I am doing a new thing! Now it springs up; do you not perceive it? I am making a way in the wilderness and streams in the wasteland. –
Isaiah 43:19

DAY FIFTEEN: ACTION

Action – from Latin actionem *(nominative* actio*) "a putting in motion; a performing, doing"*

The Matthew account of the Advent adventure begins with a genealogy. Big yawn. Lists of names do not excite me. However, immediately after this list events start spinning.

The angel appears to Joseph in a dream and "When Joseph woke up, he did what the angel of the Lord had commanded…" No hesitation. Right into action.

In Luke's account Gabriel tells Mary of Elizabeth's pregnancy, and "… Mary got ready and hurried to a town in the hill country of Judea, where she entered Zechariah's home and greeted Elizabeth." Bam! Straight at it.

Even John *in utero* gets into the swing of things: "When Elizabeth heard Mary's greeting, the baby leaped in her womb." Nobody here is dawdling about.

The narratives race along leaving us breathless. Yet in reality each of these events took time. Joseph did what the Lord commanded immediately, but there would have been days, perhaps weeks before all the preparations and customs of the time would have allowed him to bring Mary into his home.

Mary hurried to Judea, but that journey would have taken anywhere from three to five days.

So while no one is lollygagging around, the very facts of their lives would give them plenty of time to consider their actions. People took time to think in first century Palestine because they had no other choice.

Our modern Advent celebration entails a strange compression of time. The original events (including Gabriel's appearance to Zechariah) took no less than fifteen months. Our Advent celebration takes four weeks. No wonder we're in a rush! Christmas preparations seem to go by in a whirlwind. We race from one activity to the next: shopping and plays and concerts and parties and visits and... And when Christmas is over we heave an exhausted sigh of relief. There is something deeply wrong with this picture.

The first Advent was filled with action but not with frantic activity. None of the players raced from pillar to post, cramming their hours with ever more events. And, I suspect, as a result, when that first blessed "Christmas" day came the only sighs were sighs of joy.

My prayer today is that I will seek to carve out unnecessary activity and instead fill this Advent season with joyous anticipation.

In vain you rise early and stay up late, toiling for food to eat—for he grants sleep to those he loves. – Psalm 127:2

DAY SIXTEEN: GATE CRASHERS

*Guest – from Proto-Indo-European root *ghos-ti- "stranger, guest; host" (cognates: Latin* hostis *"enemy,"* hospes *"host" -- from* *hosti-potis *"host, guest," originally "lord of strangers")*

In so many ways the Christmas season is about family. From the fiercely commercial (and bribery) aspect of children seeking gifts from their parents (with or without Santa) to the traditional picture of the whole tribe gathered around the table for the Christmas dinner, we see this time as being family-centric.

However, there is another side to Christmas: the whole notion of good will toward all. We are more prone to philanthropy in the Christmas season than at any other time of year. Charities receive generous donations, soup kitchens are copiously provided for, often with more volunteers than they can handle.

Something about that original Gift from God inspires our hearts to open—even those hearts that do not believe in Him. "Scrooges" truly are rare in this season.

The last thing Mary, exhausted from giving birth, and Joseph, concerned with the welfare of his young family, expected was an invasion of shepherds. Wasn't it enough that they had to bed down with the animals? Now this!

Unexpected visitors are so often mildly disconcerting—not least because they rarely seem to arrive at a convenient time. We don't know how long it took for the shepherds to get from the fields to the Messiah. Even if it was the next afternoon before they arrived, Mary and Joseph would certainly not be expecting guests. And they would have had to make some effort at hospitality. (Picture a frazzled Joseph running to the innkeeper, asking for wine and bread for his guests.) It was the culture; it was expected; it was necessary. Their meager "home" would have to become a receiving center for anyone God sent their way. Eventually that would include wealthy magi—again showing up unexpectedly. (Now picture Mary in a housecoat, a rag tied around her hair and a mop in her hand, opening the door to an assortment of richly garbed foreigners.)

We never know whom God plans to send to our doorstep, but we, like Mary and Joseph, need to welcome each one graciously, pondering what God has in mind for our interaction with them, offering good will to all.

My prayer today is that I will have an open heart and an open home to whomever God sends my way.

Do not neglect to show hospitality to strangers, for by this some have entertained angels without knowing it. – Hebrews 13:2

DAY SEVENTEEN: HERE AND NOW

When I fully enter time's swift current, enter into the moment with the weight of all my attention, I slow the torrent with the weight of me all here
— Ann Voskamp, One Thousand Gifts

In the rush to Christmas, the preparations for the holiday to come, it is too easy to find ourselves carried along by the madness of the "silly season." The never-ending to-do list, gifts to buy, food to cook, cards to write, a tree to buy and decorate. Trips to the post office, the mall, the grocery store, the salon, the Christmas bazaar, children's plays, church cantatas, parties. And suddenly Christmas is upon us, and we are unprepared, unrested, unconsecrated.

Where went Advent? Where went the soulful consideration of the King to come? And how can we stop this rollercoaster? In the midst of it all, meals must be prepared whether sumptuous feasts or simple morsels, barked shins must be soothed and scraped knees bandaged. It is not just a matter of choosing what to do and when to simply say "no" (although that may be part of the answer).

Can I *be* in the moment, see God in the moment, during the moment? Can I seek God's presence in the bread pan and dishpan? Can I look for the Christ child while I roll out the gingerbread men? Can I be present to the greatest Gift as I wrap gifts?

Perhaps the secret is not in finding time, not in making time, not in saving time, but in redeeming time. Seeing the clock and calendar not as the enemy but as the opportunity. I have this time—these moments while I clean this turkey—to seek the face of God. Perhaps the secret is in making the holidays holy days so that we are conscious of God-with-us in the middle of the mundane and the frenzied.

My prayer today is to see God not just present at the end of Advent but present in my preparations for His coming.

God did this so that they would seek him and perhaps reach out for him and find him, though he is not far from any one of us. "For in him we live and move and have our being." – Acts 17:27-28(a)

DAY EIGHTEEN: THINKING IT THROUGH

Ponder – from Latin ponderare *literally "to weigh"*

Ah, Mary. How did you take in the enormity of what was presented to you, the astonishing events of your pregnancy and the birth of your Spirit-child? How could you do anything but ponder? It was so amazing.

You didn't blab to everyone around. You didn't ask your friends and family for advice. You simply held onto things and pondered them in your heart. What faith, what trust you must have had to simply accept and believe what God had told you.

I do wonder about the nature of your ponderings though. Were you asking questions of yourself? Were you asking questions of God? Were you thinking about the future and what God's words might bring?

We worry, if we're smart, about navel gazing. We don't want to waste time in narcissism, focusing on what's going on inside us to the detriment of those around us. That's a good thing. And I doubt that Mary was considering her own self, life or emotions exclusively.

But perhaps we don't do enough pondering in our lives. We are quick to spew out our thoughts on all manner of social media. Yet there is a weight to the events of our lives, to how we spend our days and nights, that somehow gets lost in the sharing. Some things need to be taken out, turned over, put on the balance and declared worthy or worthless in front of no one but ourselves and God.

Perhaps we need to spend time considering the things that God has put into our lives. The things that He has told us, gifts He has given us, even if those gifts seem awkward and difficult. Consider them, hold them before my eyes and God's alone, and hear what He has to say.

My prayer today is that I will take time to ponder the things that God has put into me.

But Mary treasured up all these things and pondered them in her heart. – Luke 2:19

DAY NINETEEN: TRAVELING MERCIES

Travel – "to journey," from travailen *"to make a journey," originally "to toil, labor"*

I remember when I was a child someone once said that Jesus couldn't have been born in December because God would not have made Mary and Joseph make the trip during harsh weather. (Theological issues aside, I don't know that the weather in Israel would actually compare with the sub-zero temperatures we were experiencing.) The reality, of course, is that God could have chosen any number of ways to make the birth of His Son easier—for starters, not choosing a single woman and all the rumor and speculation that had to have surrounded what would clearly have been seen as infidelity and illegitimacy.

He could have chosen a time that would not require Mary and Joseph to travel when she was pregnant or a scenario in which Jesus was born in a more comfortable setting than a stable.

He didn't. God allowed—even arranged—the time and place of Jesus' birth. Whatever time of year it was, the fact is that Jesus' arrival was accompanied by discomfort upon discomfort. We don't know exactly when Mary and Joseph travelled from Nazareth to Bethlehem or how long the journey took or how long they were in Bethlehem before Jesus' birth. But whether she was in the sixth month or just days before delivery, the journey (whether riding a donkey, in a cart or on foot) could not have been entirely pleasant.

Long days, dusty roads, the pressure of an imperial dictate. Concern over the baby, concern over the situation to come. (Would Joseph's relatives have room for them? Would they be able to register before the baby came?) Concern over the situation they'd left. (Questions about Mary's reputation and Joseph's standing in the community.) The journey itself had to be filled with stress and uncertainty. And yet...

As they gazed into the starry blanket of the sky they could grasp the memories of the angelic assurance that God was in control. They could hold onto the conviction that He was with them as the miracle Immanuel-child grew and moved within Mary's womb. They traveled with the certainty that although the journey was not easy, the God who had called them would be faithful to bring them to their destination. His mercies were within reach, new every morning.

My prayer is that in the midst of my journey, I will grab hold of the truth of God's presence with me on the way.

...being confident of this, that he who began a good work in you will carry it on to completion until the day of Christ Jesus. – Philippians 1:6

DAY TWENTY: COMING AND GOING

Incarnation – from Latin incarnationem *"act of being made flesh" (used by Church writers especially of God in Christ)*

What was it like, going from infinity to just a few cells growing in Mary's womb? How can we even begin to comprehend all You gave up, Jesus, when You said, "Yes" to the Father and clothed yourself in flesh? Not just the flesh of a person (as when You visited with Abraham, when You wrestled with Jacob), but the flesh of a baby, helpless and ignorant? What did You know in the womb, in the "secret place"? Did You know then who You were? Did You remember what You'd left?

When You were outside of time, the "future" (linear, human concept that it is) was clear to You. You saw not just the final torture of the cross, but the years of stubbed toes and colds and skinned knees of the human body that would be Yours. You knew what was coming, and yet You chose to leave the perfection of heaven and come here anyway, blessed Lord.

You saw the unrequited adolescent crushes, the daily betrayals of thoughtless friends, the taunts of bullies that would assail Your human heart, the loss of Your foster father, perhaps the deaths of beloved friends and family, and Your departure, the human severing from the ones who would become Your faith family. You saw not only the joy of the reunion to come in heaven, but also the grief You would feel here on earth. You saw it all, and still You chose to leave infinite, joyous communion with the Father and the Spirit and to come live among us.

What was it like, Creator of all things, to become "created," to step from infinity into time and space, to limit yourself to frailty and the vagaries of human thought, to know that, at least for a time, You would have no knowledge of Your true identity? How did it feel to know that You, just like the rest of us, would have to grow into the realization of who You were and why You were here, knowing that You, too, would feel the frustration and confusion—for a time—of seeking to understand Your place in the world?

And yet, seeing it all, for the sake of love You chose to step down from Your throne, take off Your "God clothes" and wrap yourself in flesh.

My prayer today is that I will choose the best thing—even when it is the hard thing—for the love of those around me.

For this reason he had to be made like them, fully human in every way, in order that he might become a merciful and faithful high priest in service to God, and that he might make atonement for the sins of the people. Because he himself suffered when he was tempted, he is able to help those who are being tempted. – Hebrews 2:17-18

DAY TWENTY-ONE: EYES WIDE OPEN

Seek – from Proto-Indo-European from root *sag- *"to track down, seek out"*

This Advent adventure is one of expectation, not simply of waiting but of *awaiting*, looking out for something specific. The shepherds kept watch, protection against predators, eyes piercing the landscape for a furtive movement, an unfamiliar shadow, an unwelcome visitor. The magi watched the skies, probing for any new sight, a change in the starscape heralding portents of good or evil, or so they believed.

All these eyes were keen to see changes, sharp for what might come. One thing the shepherds were not looking for was an angelic visitation.

So often as we watch and wait, what comes to us is completely unexpected. Eagle-eyed, we search for what is to come, for what has been promised, and we are blindsided by what actually shows up. We keep watch for peril and instead find glory. We seek stars and find babies. God has a wonderful way of sneaking up on us unawares. How can a God big enough to create the universe sneak? He is mystery, pure and simple.

No matter how diligently we watch, what we find is always a surprise. This is what makes an adventure—not what we expect, but what is unexpected.

My prayer today is to embrace the unexpected in this Advent adventure.

And there were shepherds living out in the fields nearby, keeping watch over their flocks at night. – Luke 2:8

DAY TWENTY-TWO: STEP BY STEP

Step – from Proto-Indo-European root *stebh- "post, stem; to support, place firmly on"

The Advent adventure is BIG. Angelic visitations, exciting dreams, high drama. God is getting our attention in a major way. He is stepping out of heaven, stepping out of His apparently remote existence and breaking into our world. Signs, wonders, miracles. This is news-worthy stuff. God is taking His humble servants on the ride of a lifetime.

But wait. These folks are just that: humble servants, each and every one. No big names (at least not yet), no high-power positions, no dramatic life reversals. As far as we know not one of the players in the Advent story lived a "rock star for God" lifestyle. True, we don't know anyone's back story here. We don't know how many times Mary or Joseph or Elizabeth or Zechariah stumbled before they were ready to heed God's big call for their lives. We only know that they were average people going about their average lives. Yet when God's time came for the miraculous, their hearts were willing.

Their giant leaps of faith came on the heels of lives filled with small, plodding, daily steps of faith. One decision at a time, choosing to obey, to draw near, to seek grace. Each one found him or herself ready—no, certainly not expecting, but ready—to take the leap God asked them to take only because he or she had laid the foundation by those daily, mincing steps.

Had they blown it at any time before? Had they misstepped or chosen unwisely or not thought through consequences? Certainly; they were, after all, human. Their leaps of faith grew out of lives lived in the daily battle of decisions, stumbles, knocks, and regroupings that make for maturity. They learned to take small steps, and then, one by one, took them until the day when God presented the miraculous.

My prayer today is that I will choose to take those small steps in the right direction until I reach God's destination.

Who dares despise the day of small things… – Zechariah 4:10a

DAY TWENTY-THREE: MIRACLES

Miracle – from Latin mirari *"to wonder at, marvel, be astonished," earlier* smeiros, *from Proto-Indo-European* smei- *"to smile, laugh"*

What is it that makes this time of year so special? A baby? A manger? Wise men and stars? Friends and family? Waiting and hoping? Even the world that does not embrace the coming King grabs hold of this celebration. They look past the one Gift and make this a time for many gifts, a time of good will toward men—even toward those with whom God is not so pleased. The world has built up its own mythology around Christmas, but it all started with a miracle. It all started when Mary said, "Be it unto me…"

Every new life is a tiny taste of miracle. Whether daffodil or kitten or sunrise or human babe, any time something that was *not* suddenly bursts forth, God shows His power and is glorified. When God saw all He had created and declared it good, did He smile? I'll bet He did! When a star flames into being, God smiles and wise men marvel. If we are wise, we smile when God smiles.

The Christ child was miracle personified. His birth place prophesied from ancient times, His divine conception, His birth heralded by angels, worshipped and lauded in the manger and cradle. Every aspect of His coming shouted out, "Miracle!" And God smiled and we smile and all is good.

My prayer today is that I will see, truly see, the miracles around me with God's eyes, and so, then I will smile when God smiles, laugh when God laughs and be astonished.

After the people saw the sign Jesus performed, they began to say, "Surely this is the Prophet who is to come into the world." – John 6:14

DAY TWENTY-FOUR: OPEN ARMS

Take myself, and I will be ever, only, all for thee – Frances Ridley Havergal, "Take My Life and Let It Be"

It's coming closer. Can you hear it, see it, smell it? The time is nearly upon us, anticipation throbbing in our hearts. Everything is ready: the house decorated, the presents wrapped, stockings hung by the chimney with care (either literally or figuratively). Christmas is just a heartbeat away.

My favorite Christmas tradition—from the time I was a young teen until well into my thirties—was attending a Christmas Eve candlelight service. The carols, the scent of wax and the flicker of candles on the altar. Then the sanctuary lights dim as "Silent Night" is softly sung, and one candle is lit from the flame of the Christ candle. And from that another and another and another until the whole sanctuary is bright and our hearts are ablaze with the love and sanctity of this moment.

After the service ended I never wanted to extinguish my candle, never wanted the lights to come up and allow life to return to its noise and bustle. Christmas Eve, with its sense of quiet anticipation, somehow feels even more sacred than Christmas Day. During this moment of holiness, before the manic rush of avarice sets in, I can sense God reaching out, reaching down, opening His arms and calling me to come and rest in His love. In this moment I believe I will do anything for Him, and I know He has done everything for me. He has gladly left eternity for me. He has orchestrated the very universe to herald this night and what it will bring.

A new-born King, a sea change, Love all loves excelling. In this one act He opens His arms and welcomes us. Can you sense it? Do you feel it?

My prayer today is that I will not only *believe* I will do anything for Him, but that I *will* open my arms to His embrace and do anything He asks, today and every day.

But when the set time had fully come, God sent his Son, born of a woman, born under the law, to redeem those under the law, that we might receive adoption to sonship. – Galatians 4:4-5

CHRISTMAS DAY
O HAPPY DAY

Christmas – from Greek khristos *("the anointed") + mass from Late Latin* missa, *fem. past participle of* mittere *"to let go, send"*

Every good story, even in real life, has a climax—the point to which all the previous events lead. And so we reach it today. As is always the case, there will be other climaxes: the baptism, the cross, the resurrection, the Last Day. But today is the fulcrum upon which events balance. Every day from here on will be built upon this one event, a birth, a new start, a genesis. The Advent adventure is over, and the next adventure is just beginning. Mary and Joseph, Elizabeth, Zechariah and baby John, the shepherds, the wise men and evil King Herod—all their lives are changed forever because of this one day in time. And you and I, too, live lives altered by this slice of life.

It's true; the shepherds could return to their sheep and only occasionally recall their amazing angelic visitation and the hasty trip to Bethlehem, bringing it up in their old age like a legend or a rumor. The magi could return to the East and continue searching the skies for whatever else they might portend. Even the new parents (old and young) could simply move into the routines of family life.

Or they could all change radically, dramatically and permanently. All the players in this drama could spend the rest of their lives proclaiming the wonder of what God had done for them, with them, through them.

I wonder, were the shepherds among the crowds who welcomed the adult Jesus into Jerusalem? Were the wise men some of the foreigners gathered at Pentecost? Were some of Jesus' followers people who had heard the stories of these climax witnesses?

After the tree is taken down and the last morsels of Christmas leftovers are eaten, I could pack away the celadon Thai nativity set that graces my living room, tuck God-with-us into the spare room and live as if I had taken no part in this Advent adventure, returning to life as usual. Or…

We were therefore buried with him through baptism into death in order that, just as Christ was raised from the dead through the glory of the Father, we too may live a new life. – Romans 6:4

ABOUT THE AUTHOR

Celeste Allen is a writer, retreat leader and the host of The Oaks Oasis, a retreat house in Italy for people in Christian ministry. She has been involved in Christian work for more than twenty years, first in short-term missions teaching in Asia with English Language Institute/China, then serving full-time with Frontiers in the United Kingdom. Along with her spiritual formation group, The Eshcol Community, Celeste leads retreats for missionaries from around the world. If you would like more information about Celeste's ministry, you can reach her via email at TheOaksOasis@gmail.com.

Made in the USA
Middletown, DE
20 November 2014